# Pembrokeshire:
# its present and past explored

## J. Geraint Jenkins

First published in 2016

© text: J. Geraint Jenkins
© publication: Gwasg Carreg Gwalch 2016

ISBN: 978-1-84524-246-6

Cover design: Eleri Owen
Photographs: Gwasg Carreg Gwalch
Pierino Algieri p111
Boat trips and marine wildlife photos:
Janet Baxter and Lyndon Lomax

Published by Gwasg Carreg Gwalch,
12 Iard yr Orsaf, Llanrwst, Wales LL26 0EH
tel: 01492 642031
email: llanrwst@carreg-gwalch.com
website: www.carreg-gwalch.com

**J. Geraint Jenkins**

*The author (1929-2009) was a rural life and maritime academic who spent his career promoting this Welsh heritage in a lively and careful way at the National Folk Museum St Fagan's and the Welsh Industrial and Maritime Museum in Cardiff's docklands. A prolific author who researched his fields of interest with meticulous care, he was also a popular lecturer and very good company.*

*Page 1: Caerfai cove near St David's;*
*opposite: Bosherton cross*
*Page 5: window of Tudor Merchant House*

COMPACT
CYMRU

# Pembrokeshire:
## its present and past explored

### J. Geraint Jenkins

*Pembrokeshire explored*

# Contents

# Introduction

Pembrokeshire is a peninsula that projects into the Celtic Sea, and just like Llŷn in northern Wales, it has from the dawn of civilisation provided a landing stage for migrating people. Many of these groups from the European Continent and travelled the coastal sea routes of Western Europe. Wave upon wave of people through the Neolithic, Bronze and Celtic ages, from Viking invaders to Norman colonialists and from Irish immigrants to Flemish Weaves, all came and each group left an indelible mark on the landscape and life of this western outpost. No part of Pembrokeshire is further than eight miles from the sea or a waterway, and seafaring and trading has always figured prominently in the history of the area.

Dominating the county is the estuary of the two Cleddau rivers that stretches from St Anne's Head on the western coast for about ten miles penetrating the heart of the county. Throughout the ages the Haven was a scene of considerable activity not only for the industrial development along its shores but also as a centre of maritime activity offering 'the only perfect and accessible shelter from all winds at all times and for all classes of vessels between Falmouth and Holyhead'. In 1946 it was described as the best and most foolishly neglected harbour in Europe.

For over a thousand years, the county of Pembroke was distinguished by an unseen frontier – the Landsker – that separates the north of the county from the south. The Landsker is by tradition, a linguistic and social boundary that separated the predominantly Welsh speaking north from the Norman gained lands, the territory 'Down Below'. The southern land of green fields and gentle slopes, of spectacular limestone cliffs and sheltered creeks with spectacular Norman castles and castellated churches is unique. Added to the Anglo-Saxon and Viking place-names and remarkable natural beauty and one has a region with its own character and personality that has attracted man from the earliest times to the 21st century.

The landscape of northern Pembrokeshire

*Porth Mawr (Whitesands Bay) and the islands near St David's from Carn Llidi*

is dominated by the rolling hills of the Preseli a bastion of the Welsh language and tradition, whose history may be traced back to prehistoric times. Throughout the centuries its inhabitants have contributed greatly to the culture of Wales and the area has supported many poets of national repute, literary figures and musicians. It still remains a stronghold of the Welsh language and culture. Many of its farms have been occupied by the same families over many generations and continuity is the keynote to the understanding of the Preseli communities. Moreover the villages of northern Pembrokeshire have not witnessed the immigration of alien people on the scale of other areas in western Wales. Villages such as Crymych and Rosebush, Maenclochog and Mynachlog-ddu have retained their Welsh character, personality and language despite the erosion of many traditions with the influx of strangers. Many of those strangers that have settled in the area have soon appreciated the culture of the society and it is of some significance that a number of people awarded the prestigious award of 'Welsh Learner of the Year' have been residents of Preseli villages. Of course over the centuries the people of the Preseli have received much; the area has witnessed many invasions and influences, but its core of Welshness has remained as a beacon over the centuries.

The northern coast of Pembrokeshire consists largely of high cliffs open to the storms of the Atlantic, but here and there, swiftly flowing streams from the hills provide a routeway from the sea to the interior. Some of those rivers such as the Gwaun has no estuary and the river flows through a deeply entrenched gorge-like valley where human habitation is scarce. Like old remote areas, old traditions and old habits have persisted in the Gwaun valley. Here, the Old New Year (*Calan Hen*) still persists and domestic beer brewing is still practiced in many of the remote farmbuildings and cottages.

Many of the northern seaside villages of Pembrokeshire were once heavily involved in the maritime trade and Newport (*Trefdraeth*) was a notable shipbuilding and trading centre while Fishguard (*Abergwaun*) and Goodwick (*Wdig*) were developed into the packet station to Ireland and has dreams of becoming a

*1. Abercastell; 2. 'The Green Bridge of Wales'; 3. Bullslaughter; 4. Tenby beach*

centre of the Trans-Atlantic passenger trade. Cunard lines such as the *Mauretania* and *Lusitania* were no strangers to Fishguard before the First World War.

It was the distinguished Professor E.G. Bowen for many years the Head of Geography and Anthropology in Aberystwyth who wrote:

'The study of any area which has had a long history of human settlement shows quite clearly that the cultural landscape contains many elements besides those associated with the present day life of its inhabitants. The cultural landscape of such an area has been compared with an ancient manuscript that has been written over on several occasions, yet parts at least of the different writings can still be made out at the present time. Much of the landscape of a settled country like Wales is that a veritable palimpsest of culture.'

*A standing stone on the Preseli hills*

This is certainly true of southern Pembrokeshire that bears witness to many generations from the past. Immigrating people came to the area and left an indelible mark on the land and its people. Neolithic farmers came from lands across the sea in their skin-covered boats and dug-outs

*Golden gorse and sunshine on the Preseli*

and were widely involved in trade around the shores. Tombs and ceremonial centres were constructed by the Neolithic and Bronze Age settlers are commonplace in southern Pembrokeshire. Far more common havens are the settlements of the Iron Age invaders who settled in the area and lived within stockaded ramparts. The Roman influence on the lower part of the county was not great, but the area was often visited by the Viking invaders who left their mark on the many Scandinavian place-names of the area. The Normans and the English built their elaborate castles occupied by 6 people foreign in speech and customs dominated the landscape. Haverfordwest (*Hwlffordd*) and Tenby (*Dinbych y pysgod*), Pembroke (*Penfro*) and Manorbier (*Maenorbŷr*), Carew end and Lamphey are all settlements built around a castle. Many other people from pirates and smugglers, industrial workers and tourists have all come to southern Pembrokeshire and the many visitors to the areas, even the tourists of the 20th century ensured its virtual disappearance of the Welsh language amongst its people.

In the first decade of the 21st century,

the Welsh language became far more important in the life of the people of the anglicised part of the county. A flourishing bilingual 3-16 school was established in Haverfordwest and a new Welsh language local newspaper *Below the Landsker* was launched. As in the thousands of years that passed from Neolithic times, this most beautiful and varied county has witnessed many changes and has welcomed many people from other parts of Europe and beyond, but has also retained its native and very special character.

*Carreg Waldo – a memorial to Preseli's premier poet in the 20th century; above: cairns*

# Early Civilisation

For thousands of year before the arrival of the Roman invaders settlers and traders utilised the sea routes of the Western Approaches. The peninsulas of Brittany and Cornwall, Dyfed and Llŷn as well as the seaways to Ireland were extensively used by the earliest sea-going men as they sailed these familiar, trans-peninsular routes in search of trade. The vessels used by those early seafarers were probably made of animal skins stretched tightly over a wooden frame, the fore-runners of the modern Irish *Curragh*. Such craft had the advantages of being easily navigable, safe to land on sandy beaches and light enough to be carried clear of the tide by a few men. In the Welsh tales, the *Mabinogion*, such vessels were sea-going keeled boats that could be sailed extensively along the sea routes of Western Europe. The tools of craft and agriculture, weapons of war and ornaments and jewellery were all traded by early tradesmen and those trading links were crucial factors in the creation of a common culture around the Western Approaches. Over the course of centuries that Celtic culture was to be diluted by numerous invasions as the settlement of many people in the area. As Dilwyn Miles wrote in the Introduction to the *Pembrokeshire Anthology* (1981):

> 'For the last five thousand years, man has had a direct hand in shaping the face of Pembrokeshire for the Neolithic people brought with them a knowledge of the arts of agriculture. These people buried their dead with ceremony in great chambered tombs of which Pentre Ifan is the most splendid specimen.'

Being located on a promontory that juts out into the Irish Sea, Pembrokeshire has always been influenced by immigrants from across the seas. It forms part of the great highway of Atlantic Europe and from the dawn of civilisation until modern times it has been under the influence of people from across the sea! Here can be

*Pentre Ifan cromlech*

found the greatest concentration of megalithic monuments in Wales – *cromlechi* and standing stones erected by man – in Neolithic and Bronze Age times. It was from the Preseli Hills that some of the stones of Stonehenge itself were obtained, but whether those blue stones were transported by ice or by man has been the source of constant argument.

Undoubtedly the earliest inhabitants of western Wales were nomadic hunters who must have reached our shores in skin covered and dug-out boats. They settled around 2000 BC in coastal areas and developed trade with Ireland and the Bristol Channel more than with inland Wales. No traces of farmsteads have been found, possibly because they were built of perishable materials – wood, wattle and clay.

What does survive from those Neolithic and Bronze Age times are the tombs and ceremonial stone structures that still form a very important feature in the landscape of Pembrokeshire. Most were built on exposed coastlands where the prevailing winds would only allow sparse woodland to develop. In the Preseli hills, these *cromlechi*, standing stones and stone circles are found widely. Amongst the most notable in the hills above the river Nevern is the very impressive Pentre Ifan cromlech. George Owen in 1603 described Pentre Ifan as the most impressive stone structure he had seen, second only to Stonehenge. It was erected in Neolithic times (2500 BC to 1000 BC) as a communal burial for the dead and originally was covered with earth and stones to form a mound.

Of the other cromlechi in northern Pembrokeshire spectacular example may be seen in the hills above Newport. The cromlech, known as *Carreg Goeten Arthur* gave rise to many a mythical story about King Arthur and his court, that became such an important part of Welsh myth and legend. The cromlech *Llech y Drybedd* (Stone on a Tripod) near the village of Moylgrove (*Trewyddel*) consists of a very heavy capstone weighing many tons placed on a tripod of those smaller standing stones. The construction of this cromlech must have demanded super human strength.

In the Bronze Age the ancient trackways

*1. Carreg Samson; 2. Carreg Goeten Arthur; 3. Bedd Arthur (Arthur's grave)* of south-western Wales were travelled by early men towards Ireland in search of copper to mix with Cornish tin and later, gold from the Wicklow Hills. The round barrows so common in southern Pembrokeshire marked the burials of those who died along the ridgeways and their wide distribution indicates the settlement of those Bronze Age people over the greater part of Pembrokeshire. Iron Age settlers from about 500BC introduced settlements in hillforts and in the settlement of agricultural communities in those forts. These Celtic settlers brought with them the Welsh language.

The people of the Bronze Age in particular left an indelible mark on the Pembrokeshire landscape but after about 500 BC a new powerful group using iron implements and tools came from across the seas and the promontory of Pembroke was to receive a very large number of these. They lived their lives within stockaded hillforts. Of these numerous forts, that at Castell Henllys between Eglwyswrw and Felindre Farchog has been preserved to interpret the pastoral life of a Celtic people whose great contribution to the life of Wales was the introducing of

Celtic language, still spoken in Wales. Castell Henllys probably flourished between the 4th century BC and the 1st century AD. It is said that the Celts were a fierce warlike people and many of their chieftains lived in well-defenced forts like Castell Henllys. The contribution of the Celtic people to the life and culture of Wales was tremendous and the development of many centuries, and the invasion of many alien groups failed to erode the Celtic language and culture.

The Romans came with their all-conquering armies but their influence in Pembrokeshire was minimal and few ventured beyond their main west Wales fort of *Maridunum* (Carmarthen). By the early 5th century, the Romans had vacated south-western Wales, and the Preseli area, together with lands north of the Teifi were occupied by the Irish.

There were considerable contacts between south-western Wales and southern Ireland, and traders and missionaries moved freely between the two countries. Irishmen attained offices of power within Wales and place-names such

*Celtic roundhouses and heritage art and craft at Castell Henllys*

*Maen Maenclochog – another standing stone*

as *Trewyddel* (Moylgrove – Irish town), Heol Gwyddil (Irish road) all point to the relevance of the Irish in the life of south-west Wales. Many of the Celtic saints established churches in both countries, and it is said that even St Patrick himself was a native of south-western Wales.

After the departure of the Romans, one of the great tasks facing the native population was to drive all Irish people away and Cunedda, a high ranking officer in Roman Britain, came to Wales from Scotland around 450 AD to drive the Irish invaders back to the Emerald Isle.

From the 11th century onwards, the Normans came and left an imprint on the land in the form of castles and small towns built in the shadows of a Norman fort. Generations of smugglers and pirates utilised the seaways around western Wales and it was in Pembrokeshire that Henry Tudor and his cohort of 4000 soldiers landed at Dale in 1485 on his way to Bosworth. In that battle the Tudor dynasty. They marched to that battle under the flag of the Red Dragon, that in late centuries became the national flag of Wales.

To northern Pembrokeshire too came refugees from Flanders who contributed much to the development of agriculture

*Maen Mynachlog-ddu*

*Cylch Gors Fawr - a stone circle on the Preseli*

and industrial development in the region. In the 13th century the Flemings were a powerful force in the economic life of Pembrokeshire.

Throughout the centuries Pembrokeshire received many invasions and the settlement of many racial groups along its indented coast and deep valleys. Each group that came – Norman, Irish, Flemish, mariners and industrial developers, all left their imprint on the land and people of south-west Wales.

# Celtic Saints

The final departure of the Romans has followed by barbarian invasions of South East England that made sea crossings of the English Channel and the North Sea increasingly hazardous, the western sea routes assumed a greater importance. It was during this period that a considerable number of itinerant Celtic missionaries began to travel the seas off the western coast of Wales, bringing with them the ascetic austerity of the early Celtic church. To these early saints the sea constituted a highway rather than a barrier. This is reflected in the proximity of many churches where frail vessels could be easily landed. They built small secluded coastal chapels no more than monastic cells that in due course became churches dedicated to the memory of their founders. Perhaps the best known of these Celtic shrines is the tiny chapel of St Govan, built in a cleft in the rocks, virtually invisible from all directions. The early occupiers of that monastic cell were certainly convinced of the merits of solitude and a hermit-like existence.

In Pembrokeshire there are dedications to Brychan, Teilo, Padarn and of course David, probably a native of the area are commonplace. All these early churches were founded in an area well away from the zone of Roman occupation and that empire and its conquerers hardly penetrated west of Carmarthen. David and the other Celtic missionaries were in constant touch with other western based cultures in Ireland, Cornwall and Brittany.

It was the St David's area that figured most prominently in early Christianity and many of the churches of the area can be traced back to the days of St David himself. In its very early days, Christianity was established by the Romans and was recognised as the state religion in 378 A.D. During the 5th and 6th centuries, the full force of a monastic movement within the early church was to arrive in Wales. Pembrokeshire was to be the mainspring of the Celtic church. Itinerant Celtic missionaries utilised the western seaways from Brittany to Cornwall, Wales and

*1. Old cross, Nevern church; 2. St Govan's; 3. Storm-destroyed church, Cwm yr Eglwys*

*Pembrokeshire explored*

Ireland spending their time in prayer, worship, study and tilling the land. This was an austere and uncompromising religion and amongst those who came to Pembrokeshire were Teilo and Brynach, Meugan and Pedrig, Hernin and Cadfan were amongst the wandering missionaries who left their marks on the Pembroke landscape.

In addition to *Llan* place-names, settlements of the Celtic saints in Pembroke carried the name *Capel* as a prefix. Here Capel Degwel, Capel St Ffraid, Capel St Silin, Capel Wrw and Capel Brynach all figure prominently in the place-names of the county.

But all these are of relatively minor importance compared with dedications to St David (*Dewi Sant*) the patron saint of Wales. The church that carries his name was certainly a place of pilgrimage and occupying a sheltered position on a promontory of the sea, this was indeed amongst the most important of all ecclesiastical settlements in the land. In south-west Wales, there are more churches dedicated to St David than any other saint. He did not venture into northern Wales and north of Llanrhystud on the river Wyre in Ceredigion, St David was an absentee.

St David is said to have been born in Ceredigion around 520 A.D. He set up a religious settlement at Glyn Rhosyn, the site that was later to develop the cathedral church of Tyddewi. An abstemious, disciplined man became a saint of the Roman Catholic Church. Over fifty churches in Wales carry the name of Dewi and in the middle ages, it was believed that two pilgrimages to Tyddewi was equal to one visit to Rome. The day of his death around 588 A.D. still marks the National Day of Wales on 1st March annually. It is said that the proliferaton of the surname 'Davies' in south-western Wales reflects the importance of the patron saint in the life of the Welsh people.

*Two beautiful and decorative early Celtic stone crosses 1. Carew 2. Nevern*

# Centuries of invasions

Less welcome visitors who came to south-west Wales who came by sea were the Vikings who had little or no respect for Christianity and had no respect whatsoever to the ecclesiastical buildings that were such a part of life in the west. Between the mid 9th century until the close of the 11th century they pillaged and plundered coastal settlements and they burnt St David's at least eight time in those years. The sheltered waters of Milford Haven became their winter settlement and their expeditions to other parts of Wales were organised from there. It is said that 23 Viking ships and two thousand men wintered in the Haven in their beautiful long-ships. Nevertheless although the Viking invaders had a bad reputation as plunderers, they were also anxious to grasp opportunities to develop commercial and trading links and it is probable that a number of trading posts were established by them on the southern Pembrokeshire coast and in the Haven.

The most tangible evidence of the presence of the Vikings however lives on in many coastal place-names that are of Scandinavian origins. Islands like Ramsey, Skokholm and Skomer and coastal settlements such as Hubberston, Musseltown, Hasguard, Haverford and Melrfjordr (Milford) were named by Vikings familiar with the coast of south west Wales a millenium and more ago.

The Norman Roger de Montgomery and his armies from his stronghold in Cardigan, made his way to the richer pastures to the south of the Preseli hills and created a linguistic divide that exists to this day. It was the Normans and their Anglo-Saxon followers that left the most impressive and permanent imprint on the life and landscape of southern Pembrokeshire. The Milford Haven waterway became of strategic importance and the initial conquest was marked by defensive earthworks at such places as St Ishmael's, Walwyn's Castle and Castle Martin. More permanent stone-built impressive castles were built at such places as Pembroke and Dale. The Normans built more than fifty castles in Pembrokeshire, two thirds of which were earthworks. The stone castles were mostly sited on or near manageable waters, apart from a few frontier castles such as Roch erected to protect colonial gains in the southern lowlands. A number of towns such as Pembroke, Haverfordwest, Tenby and Narberth grew around the castles and acted as market towns and boroughs and charters

*Wiston – an early Norman mount*

were granted to this inhabitants. These were occupied mainly by English and Flemish settlers, hostile to the native population. Conquering armies and settlers to Pembrokeshire could be supplied by sea of besieged from the land.

Even a force of French mercenaries were landed near Milford Haven in 1405 as part of an agreement between Owain Glyndŵr and the French King Charles. In the twelfth century, the Flemings landed in Milford Haven. They established an alien settlement, feudal in nature and the agricultural surplus that they produced, corn, hides, and fish wool in particular encouraged the trade of castellated boroughs of such places as Haverfordwest, Pembroke, Tenby and southern eastwards through one of the most important Wales borough of Carmarthen. The chief imports were military supplies, salt, spices, wines and other luxury goods that were bought by the ever increasing number of wealthy burgesses who not only monopolised trade, both legal and illegal but were also important in the governance of the town in which they resided.

Undoubtedly the most important of all the natives of Pembrokeshire was Henry Tudor who was born at Pembroke Castle in 1457. Exiled in France this son of Pembroke landed at Dale on Milford Haven on 7th August 1485 and marched triumphantly to the Battle of Bosworth and began the Tudor dynasty that became of such great importance in the life of Britain and the world.

# Churches and Chapels

Although the influence of religion may have become diluted in the post-1945 period the evidence for the importance of Christian worship in the past cannot be disputed. At the beginning of the 21st century, less than 7 per cent of the population of Wales hold any affiliation with church or chapel. In Pembrokeshire there is evidence of intense religious activities in the past and every conceivable affiliation from Methodist to Congregationalists and from Quakers to Baptists all had their places of worship. In some Pembrokeshire villages, two chapels of the same denomination could be located within a short distance of one another. Thus in the Teifi estuary village of St Dogmael's for instance two congregational churches are still open. Today as in most parts of Wales, Pembrokeshire is over supplied with places of worship. Many congregations who had an allegiance to particular places of worship found the burden of maintenance so heavy that there

*Ffynnon Non and Tyddewi (St David's)*

was no alternative but closure. The structures that dominate the landscape, of the built at great expense are no longer of relevance as the tide of religious fervour that swept the land after the revivals of 1859 and 1904 has receded into the dim forgotten past. Pastors are far fewer in number and while many of the remaining churches have no ministers at all, many ministers have to take charge of seven or eight widely scattered places of worship. Of all the nonconformist chapels of northern Pembrokeshire, by far the most extensive are the Baptists and their early churches as of Rhydwilym and Brynberian are still open.

# The Land of Castles

Pembrokeshire possesses as many as 16 major castles and as many as 60 minor ones. The conquest of south-western Wales by the Normans and their associates isolated southern Pembrokeshire from the remainder of Wales by the construction of a string of fortified stone castles.

The Norman occupation introduced into Wales certain features entirely new to the country, notably feudal methods of land owning, large scale agriculture and the growth of towns and trade. They also introduced a new church and a new language. The Norman invaders and the anglicised lordships certainly left their imprint on the landscape and life of lower Pembrokeshire, perhaps more so than any other part of Wales. Life here contrasted sharply with that of the 'Welshry' to the north and the 'little Normandy' to the south. Of course those Norman invaders and their cohorts chose the best available land for the establishment of their centres of political administration and the establishment of small towns in the shadow of their castles. Thus the towns of Tenby, Pembroke and Haverfordwest were 'castle towns' and as such flourished under Norman rule. To many the numerous castles of Wales in general, are a symbol of the subjucation of the Welsh people are alien structures that are the stepping stones in evolution of Wales. The fact that the Normans built so many castles in southern Pembrokeshire is a tribute to the tenacity of the native *Cymry*. Today the castles of Pembrokeshire, some in pristine condition, others in ruins and major attractions along the Landsker that from the 11th century AD has dominated the landscape of South Pembrokeshire. The most complete and to many people the gem of Welsh castles is **Pembroke Castle**, for although little of the original structure remains behind its remarkably preserved outer walls standing on a rocky promontory overlooking the waters of Milford Haven, Pembroke Castle was built around 1290 by Arnulf of Montgomery, one of the many Marcher Lords that controlled so many parts of Wales after the Norman invasion. The original castle

*Pembroke castle*

was a small inner bailey that withstood a long siege by the Welsh although its defenders were near starvation within a multiplicity of circular rooms and towers and a high keep. Pembroke was built by a certain William Marshal, son-in-law of Strongbow, conqueror of Ireland. The gatehouse had a complex barbican and no fewer than three portcullises. It is said that in a room above the portcullis chamber Henry Tudor, the Welshman who became King Henry VII and inaugurated the Tudor Line of monarchs was born in 1457. Of course the branch of the Haven that extended as far as Pembroke developed a sea-going trade, primarily as a place of import of supplies for the Norman garrison, the nature of the river made us quite impossible to develop a large-scale commercial port due to the heavy mud and sand deposits. Despite the fact that such noblemen who took up residence in Pembroke attempted to create a monopoly by legislating that every cargo vessel had to discharge its cargo at Pembroke. With silting, the port owners had to surrender their monopoly, for only the smallest of ships could sail the shallow waters below the castle.

During the English Civil War the castle

was attacked repeatedly as Cromwell and the King, forces fought many bloody encounters until Oliver Cromwell in a letter of 11th July 1648 stated that:

'The Town and Castle of Pembroke were surrended to me this day being the 11th of July.' The supremacy of the Loyalists was extinguished and to prevent further trouble, Cromwell ordered the destruction of Pembroke Castle but all attempts of its destruction failed.

***Tenby Castle*** although in ruins occupies a green headland on the western edge of the walled town. The castle was part of a scheme by William de Valence to make the town and harbour at Tenby impregnable. Its Welsh name 'Dinbych-y-pysgod' (little fort of the fish) indicates the importance of the sheltered harbour as an important centre of the fishing industry. Together with Pembroke and Haverfordwest, Tenby was an important base for the colonisation of lower Pembrokeshire. The early history of Tenby Castle was shattered by numerous furious assaults by the Welsh. In 1153 for instance Maredudd ap Rhys, the sons of Gruffudd ap Rhys slaughtered the Norman garrison and ransacked the town. A few years later the redoubtable Maelgwyn ap Rhys attracted the town and in 1260 Prince Llywelyn ap Gruffudd and his army ransacked the town and port. By the mid-fourteenth century, the castle has been rebuilt on the orders of Richard III and the town was totally enclosed by a wall. Despite the fact that Tenby was given a Royal Charter in the reign of Henry IV and its trade as the most important port in south-west Wales was assured, both Royalists and Parliamentarians were very active and both demolished many buildings and reduced others, like the castle into ruins. By the dawn of the 17th century, Tenby was in a very bad state – the population was ravaged by a plague in 1651, the trade of the port declined rapidly; pigs scavenged the streets and many of its houses were derelict. By the mid-18th century, the fortunes of the town had recovered, mainly as an attraction to the west Wales of a squirearchy who built fine houses overlooking the bay. Tenby Castle, a ruin since the days of Cromwell, houses the excellent Tenby Museum on the Castle Hill established in 1878.

*Recreated historical scene and fortifications at Pembroke castle*

Apart of the castle at **Haverfordwest**, the county town also accommodates a museum and public archives. The castle dominates the town and occupies a strategic position overlooking the Cleddau and the landing places on that river. It is said to have been built by Gilbert de Clarc, Earl of Pembroke, a powerful figure around 1100 AD. From the rocky hill, the garrison had a view of the surrounding countryside and the steep slopes were enough to daunt even the bravest attacks. Only to the south west of the hill was there a need for artificial defences and the castle provided a formidable defence against all invaders.

**Manorbier Castle** was never a fortified edifice concerned with the defence of the realm like Pembroke and Tenby, but it was a large manor house and its fortifications were aimed primarily at defending the rich productive agricultural estates that surrounded it. The large limestone castle was built in the 12th century by Odo de Barri, another of the Anglo-Norman lords who dominated southern Pembrokeshire. Much of that noble castle remains intact to this day despite the depredations of the centuries, much of the medieval structure is intact and as in the 19th century the castle was 'excellently well-defended by turrets and bulwarks'. In addition to being a stronghold this was a nobleman's home with parkland and vineyard, fishpond and hazel groves. Of all those noblemen who was brought up in Manorbier 'the most delightful part of Pembroke – 'the pleasantest spot in Wales' was Gerald de Bari (Giraldus Cambrensis or Gerallt Gymro 1146-1223). Born at Manorbier he was one of the main observer and writer on life in Wales and through his literary work he provided an invaluable record of life in medieval Wales. Serving many political and ecclesiastical positions he published many scholarly volumes, the most important being the *Itinerarium Kembriae* and the *Descriptio Kambriae* the results of his travels throughout Wales accompanying Archbishop Baldwin in a recruiting for the crusades and of the 17 books in elegant Latin the two on Wales surpass all the others.

'These two accounts best reveal an impressive intellect keen powers of observation and gentle wit.'

**Llawhaden Castle**, formed one of the bastions erected by the Normans as part

*1. Manorbier castleh; 2.Llawhaden castle*

of the defences against the Welsh. It served too as a stronghold aimed at protecting the estates of the Bishop of St David's. Of course when it was built in the early twelfth century the Bishops were also powerful dominating the religious as well as the secular life of the south-western region of Wales. It was completely demolished in a Welsh uprising in 1192 and the castle was rebuilt in the 14th century.

Everywhere in southern Pembrokeshire, there is evidence of the domination of the Church and in addition to the numerous superb churches in the area, then as the remains of a Bishop's Castle not only in Llawhaden, but also at Lamphey when the remains of a superb palace remain 'The bishops considered their personal lives and spiritual responsibilities with all the comforts of a worldly country gentleman' surrounded by orchards, garden and fishponds, a windmill, two water mills and a dovecote Lamphey Palace was a centre of gracious living. The zenith of its development was the superb additions by the worthy Bishop Gower in the mid 14th century and after the Reformation the estate was given to Richard Devereux whose son Walter was created Earl of Essex. After his execution, decay set in but a rich sugar plantation who had made a fortune in Jamaica, Charles Delamotte, Mathias built a firm Georgian mansion, now a hotel on the site.

One of the most attractive of the Pembrokeshire castles is **Carew Castle** on the banks of the river Cleddau occupies one of the most attractive locations in lower Pembrokeshire. Located on the banks of a tidal waterway an outstanding and now almost unique feature of Carew is the tidal mill, whose workings depended on the impounding of the waters of a rising tide only to be released to drive the grinding machinery of a grist mill. The beautiful, well preserved castle was built about 1300 to replace the motte and bailey Norman structures. In the 15th century, a Great Hall was added to mark fine noble residence for a Tudor aristocracy. The reconstruction and expansion was carried out by Sir John Perrot said to be the son of Henry VIII. Obviously, Sir John lived the good life for the wine cellars of Carew Castle are very extensive, and the castle was really a fortified nobleman's residence

*1. Llawhaden archway; 2. Tidal mill at Carew; 3. Carew castle*

rather than merely a defensive military establishment.

**Narberth Castle** now a ruin is reputed to have been the home of Pwyll Pendefig Dyfed whose exploits are recorded in the Welsh tales of the *Mabinogion*. The castle once had five towers and a 'great deep dungeon'.

Despite being rebuilt in the early 1906 **Roch Castle** was a 13th century fortress on the Landsker and it was built on a stony outcrop, providing a fine view of the surrounding countryside.

**Cilgerran Castle** is a remarkably well-preserved Norman fortification erected in the early 13th Century. Situated in the picturesque village of Cilgerran, looming high above the Teifi valley, this imposing castle is roughly triangular in shape. Traditionally, medieval castles were designed with a keep or strong tower at the centre but Cilgerran Castle is unusual because two massive round towers were erected instead. The castle fell to the hands of the Welsh under Lord Rhys and was attacked during the Revolt of Owain Glyndŵr in 1405. Cilgerran castle features two wooden bridges, and even has a small number of rooms and passages that are just waiting to be explored. The castle is a National Trust property, in the guardianship of Cadw.

*1.Roch; 2. Cilgerran; 3. Narberth*

Pembrokeshire explored   39

# Welsh resistance to the Normans

After initial losses in the early Norman era, the Welsh population in Pembrokeshire regrouped and resisted the occupation under a series of able leaders. This secured their principal territories in the northern part of the peninsula and the Welsh renaissance of the late Middle Ages laid down the foundations of a strong and resilient culture which prevails to the modern day.

Rhys ap Tewdwr (d. 1093), was the king of Deheubarth from 1075 and in 1081, with the help of the king of northern Wales – *Gruffudd ap Cynan* – he was confirmed as an overlord after the historic battle of Mynydd Carn on the Preseli foothills. William the Conqueror made a demonstration of power in southern Wales in the same year, traversing the land as far as St David's. It is probable that the two kings met and that a peaceful agreement was negotiated. The Norman conquest of the south gathered a new momentum after William's death in 1087,

and among the territories then being over-run was the old kingdom of Brycheiniog (*Brecknock*). It was while resisting the Norman advance in this all-important approach to his own dominions that Rhys was killed in uncertain circumstances near Aberhonddu (*Brecon*). Pembrokeshire was invaded and numerous earth and timber Norman castles – 'motte and bailey castles' – were hastily built to secure footholds on the land.

In the 12th century, the Welsh defended and consolidated their territory under the leadership of Rhys ap Tewdwr's four grandsons. By 1155, only one had survived the brutal battles of the time and he – Rhys ap Gruffudd (1132 - 1197) – became known as 'yr Arglwydd Rhys' (Lord Rhys). He paid homage to the Norman king Henry II and campaigned against him as the need be. Rhys re-gained lands as far as Aberystwyth and Carmarthen and became the lord of Deheubarth (the whole of south-western Wales), but continued to think and act as an independent Welsh prince.

By the twelfth century much of

*Aberteifi – the recently renovated Welsh castle at Cardigan*

southern Wales had already been conquered and colonised by the Normans but Rhys was one of the very few native princes to recover land from them after 1155. It's common to call these invaders the English, but the anonymous scribes who wrote the series of medieval Welsh histories known as Brut y Tywysogion (*The Chronicles of the Princes*) usually referred to them as the French, which is exactly what they were. It wouldn't be until 1399 that an English King, Henry IV, would swear his oath of allegiance in English, and all the early so-called English kings after the Conquest never spoke that language at all.

Then, in the words of the Welsh chronicle, 'all the Welsh made a pact to drive out the garrisons of the French'. In 1165 Rhys joined other Welsh princes to resist Henry II's last campaign against them, which ended in disaster for the king who was forced to retreat to England. Later the same year Rhys completed his conquest of Ceredigion, capturing Cardigan and Cilgerran castles and the prince kept Ceredigion for the rest of his reign. Rhys's military activities were not confined to Deheubarth, though, and in 1166-7 he joined Owain Gwynedd in campaigns that led to the conquest of territories in north-eastern Wales. Rhys rebuilt **Cardigan castle** in stone in 1171 – the first stone castle ever built by any Welsh prince. As the 12th century drew to a close, Rhys was once again *engaged in campaigning against the crown* and the greater lords of the southern march. By the time of his death in 1197 he had been an active participant in war and politics for sixty years, and he had been the dominate ruling prince in Wales for more than forty years. Believing attack to be the surest means of defence, the old warrior resumed hostilities against his Norman neighbours, which continued to the end of his life. He died on 28 April 1197 and was buried in the cathedral church of St David's.

The Lord Rhys was almost certainly the first native Welsh ruler to patronize the Cistercians and played a crucial role in encouraging the spread of the order in native Welsh society. In 1165 he acquired the patronage of Strata Florida Abbey and endowed it generously. He likewise made benefactions to Whitland Abbey and the

*1. Rhys' memorial at Cardigan*
*2. A reconstructed 'poet' chair at the castle*

YR ARGLWYDD RHYS

Premonstratensian abbey of Talley in 1184-9. Rhys was also generous to poets, and the chronicle describes a festival of music and poetry, often regarded as the first recorded eisteddfod, held by the prince in Cardigan castle over the Christmas festivals of 1176.

# The Preseli Hills

While the south of the county of Pembroke is characterised by a gently rolling green landscape of rich soils and gently flowing rivers, the north of the county is quite different. Here the country of rolling hills, none more than 400 metres in height is an area of outstanding natural beauty of 'smooth green hills and moorland in purple and gold above wooded valleys. It is a land of isolated farms and small valley villages such as Mynachlog-ddu, Maenclochog, Rosebush and Crymych that all act as meeting places for the many virile rural communities.

To many it is a land of myth and mystery, but it still remains a bastion and stronghold of the Welsh language. In a relatively isolated area such as this, features of the past have been retained to a far greater extent than in less isolated regions such as the south of Pembrokeshire. Many features of the past in religion, custom, art, music and poetry have been retained and found expression amongst the population of northern Pembrokeshire. For instance it is an area that inspired one of the best lyrical poets of Wales – Waldo Williams (1904-71) and the humourist and poet W.R. Evans (1911-97). Many of the villages support choirs that have earned a national reputation and youth clubs that proliferate have provided many singers and actors that figure prominently in the championship lists of *National Eisteddfodau*.

The area is predominantly a Baptist area that has produced many ministers of national repute while certain forms of religious services, such as the *Pwnc* still remains an essential of religious services. In the annual festivities held in many of the chapels' congregations of adults and children recite portions of scripture almost in a monotone like a medieval chant and are then examined in a question and answer session by a visiting preacher. The chapels of the Preseli villages still remain the stronghold of this ancient form of worship.

Northern Pembrokeshire is sheep country and over the centuries large flocks of sheep have grazed the open slopes of the Preseli. The presence of so many sheep

*The colours and character of the Preseli*

supplied the woollen manufacturers of the area and the textile workers of the Teifi valley villages with its essential raw material. Since the flocks occupied an open countryside with few fences recognising the ownership of the sheep could be difficult and early on an attempt was made by the farmers of the region to mark the ownership of the individual farmer so that no confusion could occur. All the animals were marked with paint after shearing, but paint often wore out and a more permanent mark of ownership was required. The cooperation of all the sheep owners of the Preseli was obtained to mark each animal's ears with a distinct punched or knifed slit. Round holes and splits were cut to a specific pattern and the combination of ear marks made recognition possible. Sheep and lamb sales were frequent and important and sheep shearing that demanded a huge labour force was the highlight of the farming year. Farmers and their servants, shepherds and cottages joined together in a vast cooperative effort ensuring that all a farm's sheep, perhaps a thousand or more were sheared as rapidly as possible. Cooperation between all members of a rural community was vital and the system of husbandry could not be pursued without the cooperative effort. Of course shearing day on every farm was a social occasion, with perhaps a hundred or more attending and the quality and quantity of the food served was an indication of the prosperity of an individual farm. The close-knit Welsh speaking rural communities of the Preseli that persists to this day despite many alien influences and the settlement of immigrants from other parts of Britain and beyond.

Despite the art of tranquillity that characterised these hills and valleys, it was not always so, for between 1839 and 1844, the communities expressed their discontent in the so-called Rebecca Riots, a protest of a people against the iniquities of a ruling class of aristocrats and businessmen anxious to milk the countryside dry. Roads controlled by the many Turnpike Trusts were particularly hated. On the 13th May 1839 a party of men carrying sticks and sledgehammers destroyed the gate and gatehouses at Efail-wen. On the 6th June 1839 men from villages such as

*1. Pen-caer lighthouse on Strumble head;*
*2. Preseli from the south; 3. Preseli cairns*

Llangolmon, Mynachlog-ddu, Maenclochog and Llandysilio, a body of 350 men congregated. They met in a barn at Glynsaithmaen Farm not far from the village of Mynachlog-ddu to plan their campaign. The main enemy was the Turnpike Trusts, responsible for the maintenance of roads to a specific area. Heavy tolls were brought in and there were so many tollgates in south-west Wales each one charging the road users. The meeting at Glynsaithmaen decided to attack the gates. The first gate to go and that was for the second time was at Efail-wen.

'They arrived at the gate around 10.30pm: this time they were disguised in women's petticoats and bonnets with their faces blackened and wigs made of straw. The special constables who had been sworn in by the Magistrates to protect the gate fled. The gate was destroyed and the men disappeared into the darkness of the Pembrokeshire countryside.'

The movement spread from the Preseli hills to many other parts of western Wales and only were many of the hated tollgates demolished, but other features such as

fishing weirs, workhouses and many other sections associated with the aristocracy, the established church and the Tithe Commissioners and the Turnpike Trusts all contributed to the wrath of a struggling rural population. The identity of Rebecca and her daughters will never be known, but it was certainly a movement of hope and strength against the people of rural West Wales. One of their leaders was certainly Thomas Rees (*Twm Carnabwth*), prize boxer and chapel deacon buried at Bethel Chapel, Mynachlog-ddu where his headstone notes that he died in his garden while cutting cabbages although his death certificate specified asthma as a cause of death.

The Rebecca Riots were an explosion of the old custom of '*y ceffyl pren*' (the wooden horse) which for many chapel goers was widely used as a punishment for adulterers and other offenders. A horse of straw and a human effigy were carried on a bier by four men with blackened faces. The processions were known and advertised for three weeks before the effigies of man and horse were publicly burned near the home of an offender. Occasionally offenders were tied to a wooden frame and tarred and feathered by his fellow citizens.

In northern Pembrokeshire some ancient customs persisted much longer than in any other part of Wales. In the mid 19th century for instance Christmas Day marked the beginning of a three-week period of holiday (*Y Gwyliau*) when all farm work ceased. As a symbol of this a plough was carried into the farmhouse and placed under the table of the *rwm ford*' (the table room). There was a great deal of socialising in the individual farms much drinking of home brewed beer. All visitors were obliged to wet the plough before drinking themselves. Festivities continued unabated until the 12th of January – *Dydd Calan Hen* (the old New Year) that is still celebrated in parts of the Preseli, especially the Gwaun valley, although the calendar was changed as long ago as 1752.

*1. Rebecca Riots' celebration at Efail-wen;*
*2. Twm Carnabwth's gravestone*

# Rivers and Streams

The Preseli hills mark the watershed between the swiftly flowing streams that cascade northwards or westwards. Those short rivers have been in the past a source of power to many an enterprise ranging from corn mills to sawmills and from tanneries to woollen manufacturers. The most important of the north flowing streams that run to the Teifi is the river Cuch a very important centre of rural craftsmanship bowl turning and spoon carving, coracle making to clog sole manufacturing amongst the variety of activities. The southward flowing streams the most important being the Welsh and Eastern Cleddau and much more slowly moving, but their valleys were once the location of many important ventures especially woollen manufacturers. Many of the villages, such as Maenclochog, Efail-wen and Mynachlog-ddu were to a great extent self-sufficing communities and supported many of the artisans considered essential to the welfare of a rural community. Thus many of the villages supported such activities as clog and boot making, saddlers and blacksmithing.

## Coracle Fishing

On the Pembrokeshire side of the Teifi river, coracle fishing is restricted to Abercuch and a section of the Teifi beyond the confluence of that river and the Cuch. Fishing also persists on the Teifi and Cilgerran while to the south of the Preseli coracle fishing was practiced on the Eastern Cleddau until 1939. On the Teifi there were strict rules of precedence and privilege designed to prevent disputes between fishermen. Coracles who always fished in pairs are now rare on the Teifi, but half a dozen pairs still operate from Cilgerran for a limited season. In the mid 19th century the coracle men was described as:

> 'a numerous class bound together by a strong *esprit de corps* and from long and undisturbed enjoyment of their peculiar mode of fishing have come to

*Cwm Cuch and its fast flowing river*

look upon the river as their own, and to regard with extreme jealousy any sign of interference with what they consider their rights.'

Since the Teifi river and its wealth of salmon and sewin has over the centuries attracted anglers and traditionally those have felt the wrath of the coracle fishermen.

## Corn Milling

Of course with the swiftly flowing streams cascading from the Preseli, many a rural enterprise depended on the supply of adequate running water. The woollen industry and the leather making industry were all located in valley locations in profusion, but perhaps the most widespread of all county mills were well-driven corn mills. As recently as 1923 a local directory noted 54 working watermills, a tiny proportion of those that existed in the past and at the end of the 20th century at least four were in regular use.

*Old crafts and a coracle at the Pembrokeshire folk museum*

In west Wales generally, millers were not paid in cash for their services, but were allowed to keep a proportion of the corn that they retained for their own use. Of course many of the millers were farmers themselves and the corn they obtained came to feed the animals and poultry. Woollen manufacturers often bartered their products for agricultural practice usually a woollen factory like that of Melin Isaf, Mynachlog-ddu processed the wool from the hill farms, but the mill owner kept a proportion of all the fleeces brought in for processing into cloth and yarn. The proportion kept back by the factory owner was known as Y Doll (The toll) and was used to produce woollen goods that were sold at a fair or weekly market.

## Maltsers and Brewers

Northern Pembrokeshire unlike many other parts of rural Wales was never famous for its temperance movement and the supplying of malted barley was an important element in the activities of many a Preseli farm and corn mill. In many places the remains of malt houses especially the perforated tiled floors where barley was matured above the steady heat of a wood fire bear witness to the importance of malting in the Pembrokeshire economy. Some acres of Pembrokeshire notably the Gwaun Valley still produce vast quantities of beer in the farmhouses and inns of the area. *Macsi* (brewing) follows an age old recipe whereby the beer of the hay and corn harvests was weak and watery, whilst the beer of the Old New Year in January still remain a potent brew.

## Old crafts

An important industry in Pembrokeshire was the tanning industry, an industry that supplied the many clog and bootmakers and the saddlers that worked in all parts of the county and supplied essential goods to the rural population. In the 1835 for instance Haverfordwest had two tanners, Fishguard, St David's and Cilgerran had their own substantial tannery.

Of course, most of the essentials required by the community was produced within that community itself and essentials ranging from fieldgates to

horseshoes and from two-wheeled *gambos* (harvest carts) to billhocks and other hand tools could be produced locally by many blacksmiths, carpenters and wheelwrights. All the furniture for the home and utensils for the dairy and kitchen could be produced by local craftsmen. There were numerous tailors, dress-makers and hat makers and boot makers resident in the area, but there were travelling itinerant craftsmen, ready to visit the remotest farmstead. This was known as *'chwipio'r gath'* (whipping the cat).

This pattern of life in an upland area was to continue almost unchanged until the 1914-18 War and remnants of it were to remain until 1939 at least. The changes brought about in country life have been greater in the 20th century than those of the previous five hundred years. For instance in 1903 Pembrokeshire had as many as 45 woollen mills, the majority of them being dependent on the swiftly flowing streams from the Preseli hills for their source of power. By 1923 the number had declined to 20 mills; in 1947 only 10 remained. Today mills at Tregwynt and Solva are all that remain in production.

*1./2. The mill and produce of Melin Tregwynt*

# Pembrokeshire Slate

The industrial history of rural Wales is dominated by the slate industry of north-western Wales. In its day it employed thousands and certain towns and villages and seaports owed their very existence to them; 'the most Welsh of Welsh industries'. Here in the Preseli hills of south-west Wales too, the slate industry was of considerable importance though compared with that of Snowdonia it was a minnow, that produced perhaps 10 per cent of all Welsh slates. Nevertheless the Preseli hills produced fine quality slates varying in colour from very dark purple to grey and the slates were suitable for all purposes ranging from fine roofing slates to gravestones and from paving stones to hearth stones. On the whole, the quarries of Pembrokeshire remained small and the extraction of slate never led to the development of industrial towns like Blaenau Ffestiniog, Corris, Llanberis and Pen-y-groes nor did its existence lead to the establishment of seaports such as Porthmadog, Port Penrhyn and Port Dinorwic and the development of a network of narrow-gauge railway links that transported the slates from quarry to a port of export.

The quality of Pembrokeshire slate was as good as that of northern Wales slate and it is no coincidence that when the University of Wales was developing its site at Bangor in the early 20th century, it was the slate of Pembrokeshire that was selected to roof new buildings, much to the disgust of Gwynedd quarry owners whose slates could have been obtained at a much lower cost and transport charges reduced to a minimum.

The slate extraction industry here was scattered widely over northern Pembrokeshire, – many were very minor and left little impression on the landscape and society of the area. Others were far more impressive and the results of generations of working men are still visible in the landscape. For instance villages such as Cilgerran in the Teifi valley, Rosebush and Glogue are dominated by the remains of slate workings and although many attempts

*Coastal slate quarry at Abereiddi*

have been made to obliterate or alter those blots in the landscaping, they still remain as a reminder of a once important venture that drew pioneers and capital to those remote hills. The village of Cilgerran for instance had a number of slate quarries and in 1840 they produced at the the largest of their quarries at Fforest down river from the villages:

> 'Slate of such quality obtained in the vicinity of the town; every burgess having the right to open a quarry. Many cargoes are annually exported from the port of Cardigan.'

Dominated by a castle that stands on a promontory overlooking a gorge, Cilgerran was once a hive of activity. It has always been of importance as a centre for coracle fishing and remains to this day as the only legal coracle centre on the Teifi. In the past many of the coracle men were employed in one of the many slate quarries that dominated the valley sides. Due to the steep nature of the slopes the quarries of Cilgerran were small; the largest being Chwarel Plain that in its heyday employed 24 men. The owner was

Jeremiah Stephens of Glanolmarch Mansion, Llechryd who also owned a fleet of sailing vessels during the last quarter of the 19th century. *Chwarel Cefn* nearby was the largest of all Cilgerran quarries and until its failure in 1906 was responsible for producing hearthstones and dairy troughs. It was owned by John Thomas Griffiths and Abel Gower of Plas Castell Malgwyn. Other local aristocratic families, such as the Lloyds of Coedmor who owned the largest of the quarries at *Fforest*, between Cilgerran and Cardigan. A series of small quarries that made up the Forest Quarries – Cware Caernarfon, Cware Tomi, Cware Gigfran, Cware Forever and others allowed all their wastage to pile up in the river so that by 1900 the important seaway of the Teifi had ceased to exist due to the dumping of waste slates in the river and in an agreement between Thomas Lloyd of Coedmôr and two quarrymen David Sambrook and David Owens in 1876 they agreed 'to keep the quarries open free from rubbish therein' and not to employ poachers or persons of bad character'. In 1875 all was well and Sambrook and Owens

*1. Slate waste; 2. Rosebush industrial heritage; 3. Tafarn Sinc, Rosebush*

had no difficulties at all in paying the £80 annual rental to the Lloyd family. Within ten years however, the quarry was in difficulty and the quarrying firms found it impossible to pay the annual rent to the landlord. The flow of the Teifi was blocked by an ever increasing amount of slate waste dumped in the river. The slate industry of Cilgerran petered out with the closure of Dolbadau Quarry in the shadow of the castle that produced paving stones and slabs that closed in 1938. Only the remains of workshops and scars on their slopes remains as monument to a once important activity that employed so many Cilgerran men.

Amongst the most spectacular of quarry remains, though a minor ore compared with the lunar landscape of Dyffryn Nantlle and other sites in northern Wales, is the Rosebush Quarry and the adjacent Bellstone Quarry that depended on the Maenclochog Railway for its trade. By the 1890s quarrying activities had declined to such an extent that the owners of the Rosebush Quarry attempted to create a mountain holiday resort complete with boating lake and residential hotel. Built in corrugated iron, now preserved as *Tafarn Sinc*.

Glog Quarries in the eastern Preseli was equally prominent in the landscape. Glog was the largest of all slate quarrying works and when the manager of the large meirionnydd quarry at Aberllefenni came in 1867 he was impressed with the quality of the slate and the fact that the quarry had been in constant work 'without stop or interruption employing at all times from 20 to 40 men'. Throughout its history Glog was owned and managed by one family the Owens and operated until 1926 until the concentration of John Owen with lead and silver production as well as slate, the small village of Llanfyrnach was of considerable importance in the economy of south-west Wales. Perhaps it remains so with the headquarters of one of the largest haulage contractors in Wales – Mansel Davies.

*1. Abereiddi beach;*
*2. Cilgerran gorge from the castle*

# St Bride's Bay

The coastline of St Bride's Bay is among the most beautiful in Britain. With a cliff lined coastline and a number of secluded creaks together with a sprinkling of offshore islands St Bride's Bay offers much to the historians and natural historians, one of the most important of breeding grounds for a wide range of seabirds. Islands such as Skomer and Skokholm, Rathday and Grassholm not far offshore are a delight, whilst small villages, such as Marloes, St Bride's, Little Haven, Broad Haven, Nolton, Newgale, Solva and Porthglais have their own unique character and personality. Each village seems to cling to the edge of the land and the magnificent beaches acted as landing places for sailing vessels.

Of course in addition to being a hive of activity for many generations of smugglers, who landed their illicit cargoes in some of the isolated creaks, it was also in earlier times associated with the peregrinations of missionaries. Porth-glais is said to have been the landing place for the Irish bishop Elfys of Munster who legend tells us, actually baptised the infant St David. Building materials used for the construction and addition to the cathedral at St David's was imported through Porthglais. In later centuries, the Viking invaders used Porthglais as a landing place for repeated raids on the cathedral. They ransacked and burnt **St David's** on eight occasions. From the mid-9th century AD until 1100 AD the Vikings terrorized the coast of Pembrokeshire especially that of St Bride's Bay. Arriving in their splendid long ships the Vikings developed commercial and trading links, in addition to their plundering and terrorizing the countryside. The most tangible evidence of their presence are the many place-names of Scandinavian origins especially island names – Ramsey, Skomer, Skokholm were all named by the Viking invaders, familiar with the coast of St Bride's Bay a millennium and more ago.

It is difficult to believe that in this maritime paradise, that the coal mining industry was of considerable importance, and anthracite of a very high quality was

*Druidston Haven*

obtained from the shores of St Bride's Bay. Much of the coal was obtained from small, bell pits, but some like the Nolton Haven Colliery was located very near the coast and workings extended far out under the waves. A tramway was built from another mine – the Trefrân Cliff Colliery on the southern side of the superb beach at Newgale to ships moored on Newgale beach, while that from Little Haven was also exported via Newgale. Due to enormous geological difficulties, the industry around St Bride's Bay disappeared before the end of the 19th century.

Of all the coastal villages of St Bride's Bay undoubtedly the largest and that important was that of **Solva** (*Solfach*). Access to the sheltered and easily defended harbour was difficult and involved a zig-zag course up the river Solfach. It provided a refuge from the Viking invaders and in more peaceful times it developed into an important part by the end of the 16th century. The basis of its activity was trade with Ireland. It had nine substantial warehouses storing sea-borne imported goods for distribution to a wide hinterland. As many as 12 limekilns were built on the banks of the river. Solva was certainly a hive of activity in the 19th century, but that activity declined rapidly after about 1890. The coal mines closed the population declined from 1252 in 1851 but by 1901 had declined to 730. The old steamer continued to visit the port and Capt. D.J. Jenkins (my father) told me that as master of the S.S. *Florence Cooke* he brought a cargo of Blaenau Ffestiniog slate for repair to the roof of St David's Cathedral around 1923.

A notable feature of the landscape of St Bride's Bay are the number of offshore islands. The sea in between the islands is rough and dangerous and many a fine ship has come to grief in the wild currents of tides. Broad sound between **Skokholm** and **Skomer** where the tides meet to form the 'Wild Goose Race' is the graveyard for many a fine vessel that could not cope with the wild waters of the sea. **Ramsey Island**, once known as 'Ynys Dyfannog', accommodated the Dark Ages saints Dyfannog and Justinian is now the abode and breeding ground of the grey seal while Grassholm once the main breeding ground for puffins is now the stronghold of the

*1. Solfach haven; 2. Disused lime kilns on the shore; 3. The sailing club at Solva*

*Porth Mawr (Whitesands Bay)*

garnet, and it is said that at least 100,080 garnets live and breed there. **Middleholm** – or Midland Isle – 'Ynys Dewi' in Welsh, was once famous for its rabbits and vast numbers were exported from there to the industrial valleys. Each island and islet in St Bride's Bay has its own character, but the waters of the coast proved very dangerous for the seafarer. Thus in 1861 the **Smalls Lighthouse** was built with very great difficulty, but the red and white edifice erected in the mid-19th century still casts its light over a wild and turbulent sea.

1. *Carn Llidi on St David's head;*
2. *Freshwater East*

# Porth-gain

North of St David's, the undulating country was once famous for its corn, wheat and barley in particular. It is a gentle undulating countryside of cereal growing farms and small villages still as Trefin – famous for its corn mill the inspiration for the song 'Melin Trefin' by the national poet Crwys.

The 'white wheat' of **Llanrhian** (*gwenith gwyn Llanrhian*) was legendary and this part of Pembrokeshire was amongst the most fertile in Wales for the growth of cereal crops, that were exported through the small ports of the area to Ireland and elsewhere. The coast on the other hand is marked by a line of high cliffs, that once inspired another national poet Dewi Emrys to compose '*Pwllderi*'. This area between St David's and Fishguard is a remote and romantic area of great beauty with a strong sense of magic. The so-called 'Blue Lagoon' for instance a great tourist attraction at **Abereiddi** is nothing but the remains of quarry activities that located a huge hole in the ground. The rail network never penetrated the region despite the fact that the great Victorian engineer, Isambard Kingdom Brunel, had dreams of creating a trans-Atlantic port. In 1851, Abermawr became a site of great activity as hundreds of workers prepared the harbour. A wide-gauge railway leading to London was to be built, with so many geological and financial difficulties Brunet's dream of an Atlantic port to rival Liverpool were soon forgotten. Neyland on the Cleddau became the new ferry port with its main-line railway connection.

Until the mid 19th century Abereiddi and **Porth-gain** were very minor harbours where occasional cargoes were discharged. Abereiddi was reputed to be the principal smuggling port of the south-west coast and frequent cargoes of all kinds, but especially salt and wine were landed since Abereiddi was located on an exposed location open to the lashing of westerly gales. When the deposits of first class granite was discovered, a narrow-gauge railway from Abereiddi to the more sheltered harbour at Porth-gain, a mile or so away Porth-gain became an important

*A rocky headland near Porth-gain*

industrial village and its brickworks were as important as the workshop producing stone slabs for the building of pavements and bridges.

By 1929 trade had declined and in 1931, the *United Stone Firms* were bankrupt and the last cargo left Porth-gain in 1951.

1. *The harbour and its heritage at Porth-gain*
2. *The Sloop* 3. *At the quay-side*

# Fishguard (Abergwaun)

**Fishguard**, the most important and largest of northern Pembrokeshire settlements – was named by the Norsemen who visited western Wales from their bases in Ireland likened the old Welsh settlement of Abergwaun to a 'Fish-Yard' when the Normans came from Devon to occupy this area under Robert Fitzmartin, it is said that the natives gathered on the high ground rolling large boulders on the Norman ships.

The town of Fishguard is divided into three parts – firstly the Cwm or Lower Fishguard referred to in the past as 'Capel Llanfihangel' – the haunt of smugglers and privateers as well as a very active ship building tradition. In 1779, a privateer, captained by a notorious smuggler Stephen Manhent demanded a ransom of £500 for a merchant ship and a further £500 from the town. With the refusal of the money a bombardment of the town was undertaken by the crew of the *Black Prince* but they were sent away empty handed. As a result of this incident a fort was built overlooking the harbour. The fort was equipped with eight, nine-pounder guns it was manned by three invalid gunners from Woolwich who would have been of little use in defending the harbour or town of Fishguard.

The second section of Fishguard built on a hill overlooking the valley of the Gwaun is the modern Fishguard with its shops and hotels, places of worship and schools. It was the development of the port of Fishguard, actually located in the old hamlet of **Goodwick** that witnessed the development of the port with its connection, with Southern Ireland in the early years of the 20th century. In earlier times the fortunes of the southern shores of Fishguard Bay was developed by yet another enterprising smuggler. William Rogers, a merchant of Minehead who amassed a fortune through illegal trading with Ireland and built for himself a substantial mansion, Wyncliff which later became the Fishguard Bay Hotel.

Not far from Goodwick on Wednesday, the 22nd of February 1797, a motley army of drunken, ill-disciplined French soldiers

*The breakwater at Goodwick*